Easy and Tasty Keto Chaffle Recipes

Innovative and Tasty Ideas for Any Occasion

Imogene Cook

TABLE OF CONTENTS

Lemon Chaffle

Preparation time: 9 minutes

Cooking Time: 12 Minutes

Servings: 2

Ingredients:

- 2 tbsp almond flour
- 1 egg
- ½ apple (peeled and finely chopped)
- ½ lemon (juiced
- ½ tsp lemon zest
- ¼ tsp baking powder
- 2 tsp swerve sweetener
- 2 tbsp cream cheese
- 1/8 tsp salt

Lemon Icing:

- 2 tbsp granulated swerve
- 1 tbsp heavy cream
- ¼ tsp lemon zest
- 1 tsp freshly squeezed lemon juice

Directions:

1. Plug the waffle maker to preheat it and spray it with a non-stick cooking spray.
2. In a mixing bowl, whisk together the egg, lemon zest, cream cheese and lemon juice.
3. In another mixing bowl, combine the salt, swerve, almond flour, baking powder and chopped apple.
4. Pour the egg mixture into the flour mixture and mix until the ingredients are well combined and you have formed a smooth batter.
5. Pour an appropriate amount of the batter into the waffle maker and spread the batter to the edges to cover all the holes on the waffle maker.
6. Close the waffle maker and cook until the chaffle is browned. This will take about 5 minutes; however, the cook time may vary in some waffle maker.
7. After the cooking cycle, use a silicone or plastic utensil to remove the chaffle from the waffle maker.
8. Repeat step 5 to 7 until you have cooked all the batter into chaffles.
9. For the topping, combine the lemon juice, lemon zest, heavy cream and swerve in a mixing bowl. Mix until it is smooth and fluffy.
10. Spread the cream mixture over the chaffles and enjoy.

Nutrition:

Fat 12.1g 16% Carbohydrate 14.2g 5% Sugars 7.2g Protein 5.5g

Simple Heart Shape Chaffles

Servings:4

Cooking Time: 5 Minutes

Servings: 2

Ingredients:

- 2 large eggs
- 1 cup finely shredded mozzarella
- 2 tbsps. coconut flour
- 1 tsp. stevia
- Coconut flour for topping

Directions:

1. Switch on your heart shape Belgian waffle maker.
2. Grease with cooking spray and let it preheat.

3. Mix together chaffle ingredients in a mixing bowl.
4. Pour chaffle mixture in heart shape Belgian maker and cook for about 5 minutes Utes.
5. Once chaffles are cooked, carefully remove from the maker.
6. Sprinkle coconut flour on top.
7. Serve with warm keto BLT coffee.
8. Enjoy!

Nutrition:

Protein: 32% 52 kcal Fat: 57% kcal Carbohydrates: 10% 17 kcal

Pork Chaffles On Pan

Servings:4

Cooking Time:5minutes

Ingredients:

- 1 cup pork, minutes
- 1 egg
- ½ cup chopped parsley
- 1 cup cheddar cheese
- pinch of salt
- 1 tbsp. avocado oil

Directions:

1. Heat your nonstick pan over medium heat.
2. In a small bowl, mix together pork, parsley, egg, and cheese together
3. Grease pan with avocado oil.
4. Once the pan is hot, pour 2 tbsps. pork batter and cook for about 1-2 minutes Utes.
5. Flip and cook for another 1-2 minutes Utes.
6. Once chaffle is brown, remove from pan.
7. Serve BBQ sauce on top and enjoy!

Nutrition:

Protein: 31% 79 kcal Fat: 67% 170 kcal Carbohydrates: 2% 5 kcal

Chicken Jalapeno Popper Chaffle

Preparation time: 9 minutes

Cooking Time: 10 Minutes

Servings: 2

Ingredients:

- 1 egg
- 1 small jalapeno pepper (sliced)
- 1 can chicken breast (diced)
- A pinch of salt
- A pinch of ground black pepper
- 1/8 tsp garlic powder
- 1/8 tsp onion powder
- 2 tbsp shredded parmesan cheese
- 4 tbsp shredded cheddar cheese
- 1 tsp cream cheese

Topping:

- Sour cream

Directions:

1. Plug the waffle maker to preheat it and spray it with a non-stick spray.
2. In a mixing bowl, combine parmesan, cheddar, jalapeno, salt, ground pepper, garlic powder and onion powder.

3. Whisk together the egg and cream cheese. Pour it into the cheese mixture and mix until the ingredients are well combined. Fold in the diced chicken.
4. Fill the waffle maker with about ½ of the batter and spread out the batter to cover all the holes on the waffle maker.
5. Close the waffle maker and cook for about minutes or according to waffle maker's settings.
6. After the cooking cycle, use a plastic or silicone utensil to remove the chaffle from the waffle maker.
7. Repeat step 4 to 6 until the you have cooked all the batter into chaffles.
8. Serve warm and top with sour cream as desired.

Nutrition:

Fat 13.4g 17% Carbohydrate 1.3g 0% Sugars 0.6g Protein 46.3g

Savory Chaffles

Servings:4

Cooking Time:5minutes

Ingredients:

- 1 egg
- 1 cup cheddar cheese
- pinch of salt
- 2 green chillies, chopped
- 1 tsp. red chilli flakes
- 1/2 cup spinach chopped
- ½ cup cauliflower
- 1 pinch garlic powder
- 1 pinch onion powder
- 1 tbsp. coconut oil

Directions:

1. Heat your nonstick pan over medium heat.
2. Blend all ingredients except oil in a blender.
3. Grease pan with avocado oil.
4. Once the pan is hot, pour 2 tbsps. cauliflower batter and cook for about 1-2 minutes Utes.
5. Flip and cook for another 1-2 minutes Utes.
6. Once chaffle is brown, remove from pan.
7. Serve hot and enjoy!

Nutrition:

Protein: 32% 42 kcal Fat: 63% kcal Carbohydrates: 5% 6 kcal

Oven-baked Chaffles

Servings:10

Cooking Time:5 Minutes

Ingredients:

- 3 eggs
- 2 cups mozzarella cheese
- ¼ cup coconut flour
- 1 tsp. baking powder
- 1 tbsp. coconut oil
- 1 tsp stevia
- 1 tbsp. coconut cream

Directions:

1. Preheat oven on 4000 F.
2. Mix together all ingredients in a bowl.
3. Pour batter in silicon waffle mold and set it on a baking tray.
4. Bake chaffles in an oven for about 10-15 minutes Utes.
5. Once cooked, remove from oven
6. Serve hot with coffee and enjoy!

Nutrition:

Protein: 34% 3kcal Fat: 61% 66 kcal Carbohydrates: 5% 6 kcal

Banana Chaffle

Preparation time: 8 minutes

Cooking Time: 16 Minutes

Servings: 2

Ingredients:

- ½ tsp banana flavoring
- 1/8 tsp salt
- 2 tbsp almond flour
- ½ shredded mozzarella cheese
- 2 eggs (beaten)
- ½ tsp baking powder
- ½ tsp cinnamon
- 2 tbsp swerve sweetener

Directions:

1. Plug the waffle maker to preheat it and spray it with a non-stick spray.
2. In a mixing bowl, combine the baking flour, cinnamon, swerve,
3. salt, almond flour and cheese. Add the egg and banana flavor. Mix until the ingredients are well combined.
4. Pour ¼ of the batter into your waffle maker and spread out the batter to cover all the holes on the waffle maker.
5. Close the waffle maker and cook for about minutes or according to your waffle maker's settings.

6. After the cooking cycle, use a silicone or plastic utensil to remove the chaffle from the waffle maker.
7. Repeat step 3 to 5 until you have cooked all the batter into chaffles.
8. Serve warm and enjoy.

Nutrition:

Fat 12.5g 16% Carbohydrate 11g 7% Sugars 0.7g Protein 8.8g

Cinnamon Roll Chaffle

Preparation time: 10 minutes

Cooking Time: 9 Minutes

Servings: 2

Ingredients:

- 1 egg (beaten)
- ½ cup shredded mozzarella cheese
- 1 tsp cinnamon
- 1 tsp sugar free maple syrup
- ¼ tsp baking powder
- 1 tbsp almond flour
- ½ tsp vanilla extract

Topping:

- 2 tsp granulated swerve
- 1 tbsp heavy cream
- 4 tbsp cream cheese

Directions:

1. Plug the waffle maker to preheat it and spray it with a non-stick spray.
2. In a mixing bowl, whisk together the egg, maple syrup and vanilla extract.

3. In another mixing bowl, combine the cinnamon, almond flour, baking powder and mozzarella cheese.

4. Pour in the egg mixture into the flour mixture and mix until the ingredients are well combined.

5. Pour in an appropriate amount of the batter into the waffle maker and spread out the batter to the edges to cover all the holes on the waffle maker.

6. Close the waffle maker and bake for about 3 minute or according to your waffle maker's settings.

7. After the cooking cycle, use a silicone or plastic utensil to remove the chaffle from the waffle maker.

8. Repeat step 5 to 7 until you have cooked all the batter into chaffles.

9. For the topping, combine the cream cheese, swerve and heavy cream in a microwave safe dish.

10. Place the dish in a microwave and microwave on high until the mixture is melted and smooth. Stir every 15 seconds.

11. Top the chaffles with the cream mixture and enjoy.

Nutrition:

Fat 9.9g 13% Carbohydrate 3.8g 1% Sugars 0.3g Protein 4.8g

Buffalo Chicken Chaffle

Preparation time: 9 minutes

Cooking Time: 10 Minutes

Servings: 2

Ingredients:

- 1 egg
- 5 ounces cooked chicken (diced)
- 2 tbsp buffalo sauce
- ½ tsp garlic powder
- ½ tsp onion powder
- ½ tsp dried basil
- 5 tbsp shredded cheddar cheese
- 2 ounces cream cheese

Directions:

1. Plug the waffle maker and preheat it. Spray it with non-stick spray.
2. In a large mixing bowl, combine the onion powder, basil, garlic, buffalo sauce, cheddar cheese chicken and cream

cheese. Mix until the ingredients are well combined and you have formed a smooth batter.

3. Sprinkle some shredded cheddar cheese over the waffle maker and pour in adequate amount of the batter. Spread out the batter to the edges of the waffle maker to cover all the holes on the waffle maker.

4. Close the lid of the waffle maker and cook for about 3 to minutes or according to waffle maker's settings.

5. After the cooking cycle, remove the chaffle from the waffle maker with a plastic or silicone utensil.

6. Repeat step 3 to 5 until you have cooked all the batter into chaffles.

7. Serve and enjoy.

Nutrition:

Fat 20.1g 26% Carbohydrate 2.2g 1% Sugars 0.7g Protein 30g

Pumpkin Pecan Chaffle

Preparation time: 9 minutes

Cooking Time: 10 Minutes

Servings: 2

Ingredients:

- 2 tbsp toasted pecans (chopped)
- 2 tbsp almond flour
- 1 tbsp pumpkin puree
- ½ tsp pumpkin spice
- ½ cup grated mozzarella cheese
- 1 tsp granulated swerve sweetener
- 1 egg
- ½ tsp nutmeg
- ½ tsp vanilla extract
- ½ tsp baking powder

Directions:

1. Plug the waffle maker to preheat it and spray it with a non-stick spray.

2. In a mixing bowl, combine the almond flour, baking powder, pumpkin spice, swerve, cheese and nutmeg.

3. In another mixing bowl, whisk together the pumpkin puree egg and vanilla extract.

4. Pour the egg mixture into the flour mixture and mix until the ingredients are well combined.

5. Pour an appropriate amount of the batter into the waffle maker and spread out the batter to the edges to cover all the holes on the waffle maker.

6. Close the waffle maker and cook for about 5 minutes or according to your waffle maker's settings.

7. After the cooking cycle, use a silicone or plastic utensil to remove the chaffle from the waffle maker.

8. Repeat step 5 to 7 until you have cooked all the batter into chaffles.

9. Serve warm and top with whipped cream. Enjoy!!!

Nutrition:

Fat 14.4g 18% Carbohydrate 6.3g 2% Sugars 1.4g Protein 7.5g

Sloppy Joe Chaffle

Preparation time: 9 minutes

Cooking Time: 20 Minutes

Servings: 2

Ingredients:

Chaffle:

- 1 large egg (beaten)
- 1/8 tsp onion powder
- 1 tbsp almond flour
- ½ cup shredded mozzarella cheese
- 1 tsp nutmeg
- ¼ tsp baking powder

Sloppy Joe Filling:

- 2 tsp olive oil
- 1 pounds ground beef
- 1 celery stalk (chopped)
- 2 tbsp ketch up
- 2 tsp Worcestershire sauce
- 1 small onions (chopped)
- 1 green bell pepper (chopped)
- 1 tbsp sugar free maple syrup
- 1 cup tomato sauce (7.9 ounce)
- 2 garlic cloves (minced)
- ½ tsp salt or to taste
- ½ tsp ground black pepper or to taste

Directions:

For the chaffle:

1. Plug the waffle maker and preheat it. Spray it with non-stick spray.
2. Combine the baking powder, nutmeg, flour and onion powder in a mixing bowl. Add the eggs and mix.
3. Add the cheese and mix until the ingredients are well combined and you have formed a smooth batter.
4. Pour the batter into the waffle maker and spread it out to the edges of the waffle maker to cover all the holes on it.
5. Close the waffle lid and cook for about 5 minutes or according to waffle maker's settings.
6. After the cooking cycle, remove the chaffle from the waffle maker with a plastic or silicone utensil. Transfer the chaffle to a wire rack to cool.

For the sloppy joe filling:

7. Heat up a large skillet over medium to high heat.
8. Add the ground beef and saute until the beef is browned.
9. Use a slotted spoon to transfer the ground beef to a paper towel lined plate to drain. Drain all the grease in the skillet.
10. Add the olive oil to the skillet and heat it up.
11. Add the onions, green pepper, celery and garlic. Sauté until the veggies are tender, stirring often to prevent burning.
12. Stir in the tomato sauce, Worcestershire sauce, ketchup, maple syrup, salt and pepper.
13. Add the browned beef and bring the mixture to a boil. Reduce the heat and simmer for about 10 minutes.
14. Remove the skillet from heat.

15. Scoop the sloppy joe into the chaffles and enjoy.

Nutrition:

Fat 30.5g 39% Carbohydrate 26.2g 10% Sugars 15.3g Protein 80.2g

Cauliflower rice Chaffle

Preparation time: 9 minutes

Cooking Time: 8 Minutes

Ingredients:

- 1 cup cauliflower rice
- ¼ tsp salt or to taste
- 1 tbsp melted butter
- 1 egg
- ¼ tsp nutmeg
- ¼ tsp cinnamon
- ¼ tsp garlic powder
- 1/8 tsp ground black pepper or to taste
- 1/8 tsp white pepper or to taste
- ¼ tsp Italian seasoning
- ½ cup shredded parmesan cheese
- ½ cup shredded mozzarella cheese

Garnish:

- Chopped green onions

Directions:

1. Pour ¼ of the parmesan cheese into a blender, add the mozzarella cheese, egg, salt, nutmeg, butter, cinnamon, garlic powder, black pepper, white pepper, Italian seasoning and cauliflower.
2. Add the egg and blend until you form a smooth batter.

3. Plug the waffle maker and preheat it. Spray the waffle maker with a non-stick spray.
4. Sprinkle about tbsp of the remaining parmesan cheese on top of the waffle maker.
5. Fill the waffle maker with ¼ of the batter and spread out the batter to cover all the holes on the waffle maker. Sprinkle some shredded parmesan over the batter.
6. Close the lid of the waffle maker and cook for about 4 to 5 minutes or according to your waffle maker's settings.
7. After the cooking cycle, remove the waffle with a rubber or silicone utensil.
8. Repeat step 4 to 7 until you have cooked all the batter into chaffles.
9. Serve and enjoy.

Nutrition:

Fat 15.8g 20% Carbohydrate 6.2g 2% Sugars 2.4g. Protein 15g

Chaffle And Cheese Sandwich

Preparation time: 10 minutes

Cooking Time:5 minutes

Servings: 2

Ingredients:

- 1 egg
- ½ cup mozzarella cheese
- 1 tsp. baking powder
- 3 slice feta cheese for topping

Directions:

1. Make 6 minutes chaffles
2. Set feta cheese between two chaffles.
3. Serve with hot coffee and enjoy!

Nutrition:

Protein: 31% 56 kcal Fat: 60% 110 kcal Carbohydrates: 9% 16 kcal

Simple Chaffles With Cream Dip

Preparation time: 9 minutes

Cooking Time: 10 Minutes

Servings: 2

Ingredients:

Chaffles

- 1 organic egg, beaten
- 2 tablespoons almond flour
- ½ teaspoon organic baking powder
- ½ cup mozzarella cheese, shredded

Dip

- ¼ cup heavy whipping cream
- 1-2 drops liquid stevia

Directions:

1. Preheat a mini waffle iron and then grease it.
2. For chaffles: In a medium bowl, put all ingredients and with a fork, mix until well combined. Place half of the mixture into preheated waffle iron and cook for about 3–5 minutes.
3. Repeat with the remaining mixture.
4. Meanwhile, for dip: in a bowl, mix together the cream and stevia.
5. Serve warm chaffles alongside the cream dip.

Nutrition:

Calories 149 Net Carbs 1.9 g Total Fat 12.8 g Saturated Fat 5.1

G Cholesterol 10mg Sodium 80 mg Total Carbs 2.7 g Fiber 0.8 g Sugar 0.4gProtein 5.1 g

Raspberry Chaffle

Preparation time: 5 minutes

Cooking Time: 8 Minutes

Servings: 2

Ingredients:

- 1 large egg (beaten)
- 1 tsp cinnamon
- 2 tbsp cream cheese
- ½ tsp vanilla extract
- 2 tbsp heavy cream
- 2 tbsp almond flour
- ¼ tsp baking powder
- 1/3 cup raspberries
- 2 tsp swerve sweetener or to taste
- 1/8 tsp salt

Directions:

1. Plug the waffle maker to preheat it and spray it with a non-stick spray.
2. In a medium mixing bowl, combine the cinnamon, almond flour, baking powder, 1 tsp swerve and salt.
3. In another mixing bowl, combine the cream cheese, egg and vanilla extract.
4. Pour the cream cheese mixture into the cheese mixture and mix until well combine and you have formed a smooth batter.

5. Fold in half of the raspberries.
6. Fill the waffle maker with an appropriate amount of the batter. Spread out the batter to cover all the holes on the waffle maker.
7. Close the waffle maker and cook for about 3-4 minutes or according to waffle maker's settings.
8. After the cooking cycle, use a plastic or silicone utensil to remove the chaffle from the waffle maker.
9. Repeat 6 to 7 until you have cooked all the batter into chaffles.
10. In a mixing bowl, combine the remaining swerve and heavy cream. Whisk until you form soft peak.
11. Spread the cream cheese mixture over the chaffles and top with the remaining raspberries.
12. Serve and enjoy.

Nutrition:

Fat 30.4g 39% Carbohydrate 16.4g 6% Sugars 3.1g Protein 12g

Keto Blueberry Chaffle

Preparation time: 5 minutes

Cooking Time: 5 Minutes

Servings: 2

Ingredients:

- ¼ cups frozen blueberries
- 1 tbsp swerve
- ½ cup shredded mozzarella cheese
- 1 tbsp almond flour
- 1 egg (beaten)
- ½ tsp ground ginger
- ½ tsp vanilla extract

Topping:

- ½ cup heavy cream
- 1 tsp cinnamon

Directions:

1. Plug the waffle maker to preheat it and spray it with non-stick spray.
2. In a large mixing bowl, combine the swerve, almond flour and ginger. Add the egg, vanilla extract and cheese. Mix until the ingredients are well combined.
3. Gently fold in the blueberries.
4. Fill the waffle maker with the batter and spread it out to the edges of the waffle maker to cover all the holes on it.
5. Cover the lid of the waffle maker and bake for about minutes or according to waffle maker's settings.
6. After the cooking cycle, remove the chaffle from the waffle maker using a plastic or silicone utensil.
7. Repeat step 4 to 6 until you have cooked all the batter into waffles.
8. Combine the heavy whipping cream and cinnamon in a mixing bowl.
9. Top the chaffle with the heavy cream mixture and serve.
10. Enjoy.

Nutrition:

Fat 29.3g 38% Carbohydrate 12.5g 5% Sugars 4.4g Protein 2g

Choco Peanut Butter Chaffle

Preparation time: 9 minutes

Cooking Time: 10 Minutes

Servings: 2

Ingredients:
Filling:

- 3 tbsp all-natural peanut butter
- 2 tsp swerve sweetener
- 1 tsp vanilla extract
- 2 tbsp heavy cream

Chaffle:

- ¼ tsp baking powder
- 1 tbsp unsweetened cocoa powder
- 4 tsp almond flour
- ½ tsp vanilla extract
- 1 tbsp granulated swerve sweetener
- 1 large egg (beaten)
- 1 tbsp heavy cream

Directions:
For the chaffle:

1. Plug the waffle maker and preheat it. Spray it with a non-stick spray.

2. In a large mixing bowl, combine the almond flour, cocoa powder, baking powder and swerve.
3. Add the egg, vanilla extract and heavy cream. Mix until the ingredients are well combined and you form a smooth batter.
4. Pour some of the batter into the preheated waffle maker. Spread out the batter to the edges of the waffle maker to cover all the holes on the waffle iron.
5. Close the lid of the waffle iron and bake for about 5 minutes or according to waffle maker's settings.
6. After the baking cycle, use a plastic or silicone utensil to remove the chaffle from the waffle maker.
7. Repeat step 4 to 6 until you have cooked all the batter into chaffles.
8. Transfer the chaffles to a wire rack and let the chaffles cool completely.

For the filling:

9. Combine the vanilla, swerve, heavy cream and peanut butter in a bowl. Mix until the ingredients are well combined.
10. Spread the peanut butter frosting over the chaffles and serve.
11. Enjoy.

Nutrition:

Fat 43.2g 55% Carbohydrate 32g12% Sugars 9g Protein 19g

Avocado Chaffles

Servings:2

Cooking Time: 5 Minutes

Ingredients:

- 1 large egg
- 1/2 cup finely shredded mozzarella
- 1/8 cup avocado mash
- 1 tbsp. coconut cream

TOPPING

- 2 oz. smoked salmon
- 1 Avocado thinly sliced

Directions:

1. Switch on your square waffle maker and grease with cooking spray.
2. Beat egg in a mixing bowl with a fork.
3. Add the cheese, avocado mash and coconut cream to the egg and mix well.
4. Pour chaffle mixture in the preheated waffle maker and cook for about 2-3 minutes Utes.
5. Once chaffles are cooked, carefully remove from the maker.
6. Serve with an avocado slice and smoked salmon.
7. Drizzle ground pepper on top.
8. Enjoy!

Nutrition:

Protein: 23% kcal Fat: 67% 266 kcal Carbohydrates: 11% 42 kcal

Almond Butter Chaffle

Preparation time: 8 minutes

Cooking Time: 20 Minutes

Servings: 2

Ingredients:

- 2 eggs (beaten)
- 3 tsp granulated swerve sweetener
- 4 tbsp almond flour
- ½ tsp vanilla extract
- ½ cup grated mozzarella cheese
- ½ cup parmesan cheese
- 1/8 tsp allspice

Almond Butter Filling:

- ½ tsp vanilla extract
- 4 tbsp almond butter
- 2 tbsp butter (melted)
- 2 tbsp swerve sweetener
- 1/8 tsp nutmeg

Directions:

1. Plug the waffle maker to preheat it and spray it with a non-stick cooking spray.
2. In a mixing bowl, combine the mozzarella, allspice, almond flour, and swerve sweetener. Add the egg and

vanilla extract and mix until the ingredients are well combined.

3. Sprinkle some parmesan cheese over the waffle maker.
4. Pour an appropriate amount of the batter into the waffle and spread out the batter to cover all the holes on the waffle maker.
5. Sprinkle some parmesan over the batter.
6. Close the waffle maker and cook for about 5 minutes or according to your waffle maker's settings.
7. After the cooking cycle, use a plastic or silicone utensil to remove the chaffle from the waffle maker. Transfer the chaffle to a wire rack to cool.
8. Repeat step 3 to 7 until you have cooked all the batter into chaffles.
9. For the filling, combine butter, almond butter, swerve, vanilla and nutmeg. Mix until the mixture is smooth and fluffy.
10. Spread the cream over the surface of one chaffle and cover the with another chaffle. Repeat until you have filled all the chaffles.
11. Serve and enjoy.

Nutrition:

Fat 54.8g 70% Carbohydrate 18.4g7% Sugars 3.2g Protein 29.7g

Simple Chaffles Without Maker

Servings:2

Cooking Time:5minutes

Ingredients:

- 1 tbsp. chia seeds
- 1 egg
- 1/2 cup cheddar cheese
- pinch of salt
- 1 tbsp. avocado oil

Directions:

1. Heat your nonstick pan over medium heat
2. In a small bowl, mix together chia seeds, salt, egg, and cheese together
3. Grease pan with avocado oil.
4. Once the pan is hot, pour 2 tbsps. chaffle batter and cook for about 1-2 minutes Utes.
5. Flip and cook for another 1-2 minutes Utes.
6. Once chaffle is brown remove from pan.
7. Serve with berries on top and enjoy.

Nutrition:

Protein: 19% 44 kcal Fat: % 181 kcal Carbohydrates: 1% 2 kcal

Almond Mozzarella Chaffles

Servings:2

Cooking Time:5 Minutes

Ingredients:

- 1 egg
- 1 cup mozzarella cheese
- 1 tsp baking powder
- ¼ cup almond flour
- 1 tbsp. coconut oil

Directions:

1. Heat your nonstick pan over medium heat.
2. Mix together all ingredients in a bowl.
3. Grease pan with avocado oil and place a heart shape cookie cutter over the pan.
4. Once the pan is hot, pour the batter equally in 2 cutters.
5. Cook for another 1-2 minutes Utes.
6. Once chaffle is set, remove the cutter, flip and cook for another 1-2 minutes Utes.
7. Once chaffles are brown, remove from the pan.
8. Serve hot and enjoy!

Nutrition: Protein: 24% 43 kcal Fat: 6 123 kcal Carbohydrates: 6% 11 kcal

Bacon Chaffles With Herb Dip

Preparation time: 9 minutes

Cooking Time: 10 Minutes

Servings: 2

Ingredients:

Chaffles

- 1 organic egg, beaten
- ½ cup Swiss/Gruyere cheese blend, shredded
- 2 tablespoons cooked bacon pieces
- 1 tablespoon jalapeño pepper, chopped

Dip

- ¼ cup heavy cream
- ¼ teaspoon fresh dill, minced
- Pinch of ground black pepper

Directions:

1. Preheat a mini waffle iron and then grease it.
2. For chaffles: In a medium bowl, put all ingredients and mix well.
3. Place half of the mixture into preheated waffle iron and cook for about 5 minutes.
4. Repeat with the remaining mixture.
5. Meanwhile, for dip: in a bowl, mix together the cream and stevia.

6. Serve warm chaffles alongside the dip.

Nutrition:

Calories 210 Net Carbs 2.2 g Total Fat 13 g Saturated Fat 9.7 g
Cholesterol 132 mg Sodium 164 mg Total Carbs 2.3 g Fiber 0.1 g
Sugar 0.7 g Protein 11.9 g

Broccoli Chaffles On Pan

Servings:4

Cooking Time:5 Minutes

Ingredients:

- 1 egg
- 1 cup cheddar cheese
- ½ cup broccoli chopped
- 1 tsp baking powder
- 1 pinch garlic powder
- 1 pinch salt
- 1 pinch black pepper
- 1 tbsp. coconut oil

Directions:

1. Heat your nonstick pan over medium heat.
2. Mix together all ingredients in a bowl.
3. Grease pan with oil.
4. Once the pan is hot, pour broccoli and cheese batter on greased pan.
5. Cook for 1-2 minutes Utes.
6. Flip and cook for another 1-2 minutes Utes.
7. Once chaffles are brown, remove from the pan.
8. Serve with raspberries and melted coconut oil on top.
9. Enjoy!

Nutrition:

Protein: 20% 40 kcal Fat: 72% 142 kcal Carbohydrates: 7% 15 kcal

Chicken Chaffles With Tzatziki

Preparation time: 9 minutes

Cooking Time: 12 Minutes

Servings: 2

Ingredients:

Chaffles

- 1 organic egg, beaten
- 1/3 cup grass-fed cooked chicken, chopped
- 1/3 cup mozzarella cheese, shredded
- ¼ teaspoon garlic, minced
- ¼ teaspoon dried basil, crushed

Tzatziki

- ¼ cup plain Greek yogurt
- ½ of small cucumber, peeled, seeded, and chopped
- 1 teaspoon olive oil
- ½ teaspoon fresh lemon juice
- Pinch of ground black pepper
- ¼ tablespoon fresh dill, chopped
- ½ of garlic clove, peeled

Directions:

1. Preheat a mini waffle iron and then grease it.
2. For chaffles: In a medium bowl, put all ingredients and with your hands, mix until well combined. Place half of

the mixture into preheated waffle iron and cook for about 4–6 minutes.

3. Repeat with the remaining mixture.
4. Meanwhile, for tzatziki: in a food processor, place all the ingredients and pulse until well combined.
5. Serve warm chaffles alongside the tzatziki.

Nutrition:

Calories 131 Net Carbs 4.4 g Total Fat 5 g Saturated Fat 2 g Cholesterol 104 mg Sodium 97 mg Total Carbs 4.7 g Fiber 0.3 g Sugar 3 g Protein 13 g

Cereal and Walnut Chaffle

Preparation time: 9 minutes

Cooking Time: 6 Minutes

Ingredients:

- 1 milliliter of cereal flavoring
- ¼ tsp baking powder
- 1 tsp granulated swerve
- 1/8 tsp xanthan gum
- 1 tbsp butter (melted
- ½ tsp coconut flour
- 2 tbsp toasted walnut (chopped)
- 1 tbsp cream cheese
- 2 tbsp almond flour
- 1 large egg (beaten)
- ¼ tsp cinnamon
- 1/8 tsp nutmeg

Directions:

1. Plug the waffle maker to preheat it and spray it with a non-stick spray.
2. In a mixing bowl, whisk together the egg, cereal flavoring, cream cheese and butter.
3. In another mixing bowl, combine the coconut flour, almond flour, cinnamon, nutmeg, swerve, xanthan gum and baking powder.

4. Pour the egg mixture into the flour mixture and mix until you form a smooth batter.
5. Fold in the chopped walnuts.
6. Pour in an appropriate amount of the batter into the waffle maker and spread out the batter to the edges to cover all the holes on the waffle maker.
7. Close the waffle maker and cook for about 3 minutes or according to your waffle maker's settings.
8. After the cooking cycle, use a plastic or silicone utensil to remove the chaffle from the waffle maker.
9. Repeat step 6 to 8 until you have cooked all the batter into chaffles.
10. Serve and top with sour cream or heavy cream.

Nutrition:

Fat 18.2g 23% Carbohydrate 4.7g 2% Sugars 0.6g Protein 7.1g

Chaffle With Cream and Salmon

Preparation time: 8 minutes

Cooking Time: 20 Minutes

Servings: 2

Ingredients:

- 1/2 medium onion sliced
- 2 tbsps. parsley chopped
- 4 oz. smoked salmon
- 4 tbsp. heavy cream

CHAFFLE Ingredients:

- 1 egg
- 1/2 cup mozzarella cheese
- 1 tsp stevia
- 1 tsp vanilla
- 2 tbsps. almond flour

Directions:

1. Make 4 Heart shape chaffles with the chaffle ingredients
2. Arrange smoked salmon and heavy cream on each Chaffle.
3. Top with onion slice and parsley.
4. Serve as it is and enjoy!

Nutrition:

Protein: 34% 79 kcal Fat: 60% 137 kcal Carbohydrates: 6% 14 kcalFat: 70% 133 kcal Carbohydrates: 5% 9 kcal

Cornbread Chaffle

Preparation time: 10 minutes

Cooking Time: 12 Minutes

Servings: 2

Ingredients:

- 1 ½ tbsp melted butter
- 3 tbsp almond flour
- 1 milliliter cornbread flavoring
- 2 tbsp Mexican blend cheese
- 2 tbsp shredded parmesan cheese
- 1 small jalapeno (seeded and sliced)
- 2 tsp swerve sweetener
- 1 large egg (beaten)
- ½ tsp all spice

Directions:

1. Plug the waffle maker to preheat it and spray it with a non-stick cooking spray.
2. In a mixing bowl, combine almond flour, jalapeno, all spice, baking powder and swerve.
3. In another mixing bowl, whisk together the egg, butter and cornbread flavoring.
4. Pour the egg mixture into the flour mixture and mix until you form a smooth batter. Stir in the cheese.
5. Sprinkle some parmesan cheese over the waffle maker. Pour an appropriate amount of the batter into the waffle

maker and spread out the batter to the edges to cover all the holes on the waffle maker. Sprinkle some parmesan over the batter

6. Close the waffle maker and bake for about 5 minutes or according to you waffle maker's settings.
7. After the baking cycle, remove the chaffle from the waffle maker with a plastic or silicone utensil.
8. Repeat step 5 to 7 until you have cooked all the batter into chaffles.
9. Serve warm with your desired topping and enjoy.

Nutrition:

Fat 13.6g 17% Carbohydrate 4.1g 1% Sugars 0.8g Protein 6.4g

Midday Chaffle Snacks

Preparation time: 8 minutes

Cooking Time: 5 Minutes

Ingredients:

- 4 minutes Chaffles
- 2 oz. coconut flakes
- 2 oz. kiwi slice
- 2 oz. raspberry
- 2 oz. almonds chopped

CHAFFLE Ingredients:

- 1 egg
- 1/2 cup mozzarella cheese
- 1 tsp stevia
- 1 tsp vanilla
- 2 tbsps. almond flour

Directions:

1. Make 4 minutes chaffles with the chaffle ingredients.
2. Arrange coconut flakes, raspberries, almonds and raspberries on each chaffle.
3. Serve and enjoy keto snacks

Nutrition:

Protein: 18% 37 kcal Fat: 67% 137 kcal Carbohydrates: 15% 31 kc

Spinach Chaffle

Preparation time: 9 minutes

Cooking Time: 10 Minutes

Servings: 2

Ingredients:

- 1 egg (beaten)
- ¼ tsp pepper or to taste
- ½ tsp Italian seasoning
- 1/8 tsp thyme
- ½ cup finely chopped spinach
- ½ cup shredded cheddar cheese
- ¼ cup parmesan cheese for sprinkling

Directions:

1. Plug the waffle maker to preheat it and spray it with a non-stick cooking spray.
2. In a mixing bowl, combine the cheddar, spinach, Italian seasoning, thyme and pepper. Add the egg and mix until the ingredients are well combined.
3. Sprinkle some parmesan cheese over the waffle maker. Pour ½ of the batter into the waffle maker and spread out the batter to cover all the holes on the waffle maker. Sprinkle some cheese over the batter.
4. Close the waffle maker and cook for 5 minutes or according to your waffle maker's settings.

5. After the cooking cycle, use a silicone or plastic utensil to remove the chaffle from the waffle maker.
6. Repeat step 3 to 5 to make the second chaffle.
7. Serve chaffle and top with sour cream or use the chaffles for sandwich.

Nutrition:

Fat 14.6g 19% Carbohydrate 1.6g 1% Sugars 0.5g Protein 14.1g

Vegetarian Chaffle Sandwich

Preparation time: 9 minutes

Cooking Time: 8 Minutes

Servings: 2

Ingredients:

Chaffle:

- 1 large egg (beaten)
- 1/8 tsp onion powder
- 1 tbsp almond flour
- ½ cup shredded mozzarella cheese
- 1 tsp nutmeg
- ¼ tsp baking powder

Sandwich Filling:

- ½ cup shredded carrot
- ½ cup sliced cucumber
- ½ medium bell pepper (sliced)
- 1 cup mixed salad greens
- ½ avocado (mashed and divided)
- 6 tbsp keto friendly hummus

Directions:

For the chaffle:

1. Plug the waffle maker to preheat it. Spray it with non-stick cooking spray.
2. Combine the baking powder, nutmeg, flour and onion powder in a mixing bowl. Add the eggs and mix.
3. Add the cheese and mix until the ingredients are well combined and you have formed a smooth batter.
4. Pour the batter into the waffle maker and spread it out to the edges of the waffle maker to cover all the holes on it.
5. Close the waffle lid and cook for about 5 minutes or according to waffle maker's settings.
6. After the cooking cycle, remove the chaffle from the waffle maker with a plastic or silicone utensil.
7. For the sandwich: Add 3 tablespoons of hummus to one chaffle and spread with a spoon.
8. Fill another chaffle with one half of the mashed avocado.
9. Fill the first chaffle slice with ¼ cup sliced cucumber, ½ cup mixed salad greens, ¼ cup shredded carrot and one half of the sliced bell pepper.
10. Place the chaffle on top and press lightly.
11. Repeat step 7 to 10 for the remaining ingredients to make the second sandwich.
12. Serve and enjoy.

Nutrition:

Fat 22g 28% Carbohydrate 17.8g 6% Sugars 4.6g Protein 11.3g

Bbq Chicken Chaffle

Preparation time: 9 minutes

Cooking Time: 8 Minutes

Servings: 2

Ingredients:

- 1 tbsp sugar free BBQ sauce
- 1/3 cup cooked chicken (diced)
- 1 egg (beaten)
- 1 tbsp almond flour
- 1 red bell pepper (chopped)
- ½ cup shredded mozzarella cheese
- ¼ tsp garlic powder
- 1/4 tsp oregano

Directions:

1. Plug the waffle maker to preheat it and spray it with a non-stick cooking spray.
2. In a mixing bowl, whisk together the egg and BBQ sauce. Add the almond flour, mozzarella cheese, pepper, garlic and oregano. Mix until the well combined.
3. Add the diced chicken and mix.
4. Pour and appropriate amount of the batter into the waffle maker and spread the batter to the edges to cover all the holes on the waffle maker.
5. Close the waffle and cook for about 4 minutes.

6. After the cooking cycle, use a silicone or plastic utensil to remove and transfer the chaffle to a wire rack to cool.
7. Repeat step 4 to 6 until you have cooked all the batter into chaffles.
8. Serve warm and enjoy.

Nutrition:

Fat 11.3g 15%Carbohydrate 8.8g 3% Sugars3.8g

Protein 15.2g

Rice Chaffle

Preparation time: 8 minutes

Cooking Time: 20 Minutes

Servings: 2

Ingredients:

- 2 tbsp almond flour
- ½ tsp oregano
- 1 bag of shirataki rice
- 1 tsp baking powder
- 1 cup shredded cheddar cheese
- 2 eggs (beaten)

Directions:

1. Rinse the shirataki rice with warm water for about 30 seconds and rinse it.
2. Plug the waffle maker to preheat it and spray it with a non-stick cooking spray.
3. In a mixing bowl, combine the rinsed rice, almond flour, baking powder, oregano and shredded cheese. Add the eggs and mix until the ingredients are well combined.
4. Fill the waffle maker with an appropriate amount of the batter and spread out the batter to the edges to cover all the holes on the waffle maker.
5. Close the waffle make and cook for about minutes or according to you waffle maker's settings.

6. After the cooking cycle, use a silicone or plastic utensil to remove the chaffles from the waffle maker.
7. Repeat step 4 to 6 until you have cooked all the batter into chaffles.
8. Serve and enjoy.

Nutrition:

Fat 13.2g 17% Carbohydrate 2g 1% Sugars 0.3g Protein 10.6g

Ham Chaffle

Preparation time: 5 minutes

Cooking Time: 5 Minutes

Servings: 2

Ingredients:

- 1 large egg
- 4 tbsp chopped ham steak
- 1 scallion (chopped)
- ½ cup shredded mozzarella cheese
- ¼ tsp garlic salt
- 1/8 tsp Italian seasoning
- ½ jalapeno pepper (chopped)

Directions:

1. Plug the waffle maker to preheat it and spray it with a non-stick spray.
2. In a mixing bowl, combine the cheese, Italian seasoning, jalapeno, scallion, ham and garlic salt. Add the egg and mix until the ingredients are well combined.
3. Fill the waffle maker with an appropriate amount of the batter. Spread the batter to the edges of the waffle maker to cover all the holes on it.
4. Close the waffle maker and cook for about minutes or according to waffle maker's settings.
5. After the cooking cycle, remove the chaffle from the waffle maker with plastic or silicone utensil.

6. Serve and enjoy.

Nutrition:

Fat 10.6g 14% Carbohydrate 4.3g 2% Sugars 1.2g Protein 16.4g

Zucchini Bacon Chaffles

Preparation time: 9 minutes

Cooking Time: 12 Minutes

Servings: 2

Ingredients:

- 1 cup grated zucchini
- 1 tbsp bacon bits (finely chopped)
- ¼ cup shredded mozzarella cheese
- ½ cup shredded parmesan
- ½ tsp salt or to taste
- ½ tsp ground black pepper or to taste
- ½ tsp onion powder
- ¼ tsp nutmeg
- 2 eggs

Directions:

1. Add ¼ tsp salt to the grated zucchini and let it sit for about 5 minutes.
2. Put the grated zucchini in a clean towel and squeeze out excess water.
3. Plug the waffle maker and preheat it. Spray it with non-stick spray.
4. Break the eggs into a mixing bowl and beat.
5. Add the grated zucchini, bacon bit, nutmeg, onion powder, pepper, salt and mozzarella.

6. Add ¾ of the parmesan cheese. You have to set aside some parmesan cheese.
7. Mix until the ingredients are well combined.
8. Fill the preheated waffle maker with the batter and spread out the batter to the edge to cover all the holes on the waffle maker.
9. Close the waffle maker lid and cook until the chaffle is golden brown and crispy. The zucchini chaffle may take longer than other chaffles to get crispy.
10. After the baking cycle, use a plastic or silicone utensil to remove the chaffle from the waffle maker.
11. Repeat step 8 to 10 until you have cooked all the batter into chaffles.
12. Serve and enjoy.

Nutrition:

Fat 6g 17% Carbohydrate 4.7g 2% Sugars 1.6g Protein 20.4g

Spinach Artichoke Chaffle With Bacon

Preparation time: 9 minutes

Cooking Time: 8 Minutes

Servings: 2

Ingredients:

- 4 slices of bacon
- ½ cup chopped spinach
- 1/3 cup marinated artichoke (chopped)
- 1 egg
- ¼ tsp garlic powder
- ¼ tsp smoked paprika
- 2 tbsp cream cheese (softened)
- 1/3 cup shredded mozzarella

Directions:

1. Heat up a frying pan and add the bacon slices. Sear until both sides of the bacon slices are browned. Use a slotted spoon to transfer the bacon to a paper towel line plate to drain.
2. Once the bacon slices are cool, chop them into bits and set aside.
3. Plug the waffle maker to preheat it and spray it with a non-stick cooking spray.

4. In a mixing bowl, combine mozzarella, garlic, paprika, cream cheese and egg. Mix until the ingredients are well combined.
5. Add the spinach, artichoke and bacon bit. Mix until they are well incorporated.
6. Pour an appropriate amount of the batter into the waffle maker and spread the batter to the edges to cover all the holes on the waffle maker.
7. Close the waffle maker and cook 4 minutes or more, according to your waffle maker's settings.
8. After the cooking cycle, use a silicone or plastic utensil to remove the chaffle from the waffle maker.
9. Repeat step 6 to 8 until you have cooked all the batter into chaffles.
10. Serve and top with sour cream as desired.

Nutrition:

Fat 22.5g 29% Carbohydrate 4.7g 2% Sugars 0.6g Protein 20.1g

Chocolate Cannoli Chaffle

Preparation time: 8 minutes

Cooking Time: 10 Minutes

Servings: 2

Ingredients:

Cannoli Topping:

- 2 tbsp granulated swerve
- 4 tbsp cream cheese
- ¼ tsp vanilla extract
- ¼ tsp cinnamon
- 6 tbsp ricotta cheese
- 1 tsp lemon juice

Chaffle:

- 3 tbsp almond flour
- 1 tbsp swerve
- 1 egg
- 1/8 tsp baking powder
- 3/4 tbsp butter (melted)
- ½ tsp nutmeg
- 1 tbsp sugar free chocolate chips
- 1/8 tsp vanilla extract

Directions:

1. Plug the waffle maker to preheat it and spray it with a non-stick spray.
2. In a mixing bowl, whisk together the egg, butter and vanilla extract.
3. In another mixing bowl, combine the almond flour, baking powder, nutmeg, chocolate chips and swerve.
4. Pour the egg mixture into the flour mixture and mix until the ingredients are well combined and you have formed a smooth batter.
5. Fill your waffle maker with an appropriate amount of the batter and spread out the batter to the edged to cover all the holes on the waffle maker.
6. Close the waffle maker and cook for about 4 minutes or according to waffle maker's settings.
7. After the baking cycle, remove the chaffle from the waffle maker with a plastic or silicone utensil.
8. Repeat step 5 to 7 until you have cooked all the batter into waffles.
9. For the topping, pour the cream cheese into a blender and add the ricotta, lemon juice, cinnamon, vanilla and swerve sweetener. Blend until smooth and fluffy.
10. Spread the cream over the chaffles and enjoy.

Nutrition:

Fat 7g 15% Carbohydrate 5.7g 2% Sugars 0.3g Protein 6.1g

Keto Pumpkin Chaffle

Preparation time: 9 minutes

Cooking Time: 16 Minutes

Servings: 2

Ingredients:

- 1 cup finely shredded mozzarella cheese
- 2 tsp pumpkin pie spice
- ½ tsp ground ginger
- ¼ cup pumpkin puree
- ½ tsp vanilla extract
- 2 large eggs
- 1 tbsp almond flour
- ½ tsp baking powder
- 2 tsp sugar free maple syrup

Directions:

1. Plug the waffle maker and preheat it. Spray it with non-stick spray.

2. In a large mixing bowl, combine the baking powder, almond flour, ginger, and pumpkin.
3. Add the eggs, vanilla extract, maple syrup, cheese and pumpkin puree. Mix until the ingredients are well combined and you have formed a smooth batter.

4. Fill the waffle iron with ¼ of the batter and spread out the batter to cover all the holes on the waffle maker.
5. Close the lid of the waffle maker and cook for about 3 to 4 minutes or according to your waffle maker's settings.
6. After the cooking cycle, remove the chaffle from the iron and set aside.
7. Repeat step 4 to 6 until you have cooked all the batter into chaffles.
8. Serve and enjoy.

Nutrition:

Fat 14.8g1 Carbohydrate 9.3g3% Sugars 2.2g Protein 13.8g

Eggnog Chaffle

Preparation time: 9 minutes

Cooking Time: 5 Minutes

Servings: 2

Ingredients:

- 2 tbsp coconut flour
- ½ tsp baking powder
- 1 tsp cinnamon
- 2 tbsp cream cheese
- 2 tsp swerve
- 1/8 tsp salt
- 1/8 tsp nutmeg
- 1 egg (beaten)
- 4 tbsp keto eggnog

Eggnog Filling:

- 4 tbsp keto eggnog
- ¼ tsp vanilla extract
- ¼ cup heavy cream
- 2 tsp granulated swerve
- 1/8 tsp nutmeg

Directions:

1. Plug the waffle maker to preheat it and spray it with a non-stick cooking spray.
2. Combine the coconut flour, baking powder, swerve, salt, cinnamon and nutmeg in a mixing bowl.
3. In another mixing bowl, whisk together the eggnog, cream cheese and egg.
4. Pour in the egg mixture into the flour mixture and mix until the ingredients are well combined.
5. Fill the waffle maker with an appropriate amount of the batter. Spread out the batter to cover all the holes on the waffle maker.
6. Close the waffle maker and cook for about 5 minutes or according to your waffle maker's settings.
7. After the baking cycle, remove the chaffle from the waffle maker with a plastic or silicone utensil.
8. Repeat step 5 to 7 until you have cooked all the batter into chaffles.
9. For the eggnog cream, whisk together the cream cheese, heavy cream, vanilla and eggnog. Add the swerve and nutmeg; mix until the ingredients are well combined.
10. Top the chaffles with the eggnog cream and enjoy

Nutrition:

Fat 12.1g 16% Carbohydrate 16.1g 6% Sugars 3.4g Protein 6.9g

Double Cheese Chaffles With Mayonnaise Dip

Preparation time: 9 minutes

Cooking Time: 8 Minutes

Servings: 2

Ingredients:

Chaffles

- ½ cup mozzarella cheese, shredded
- 1 tablespoon Parmesan cheese, shredded
- 1 organic egg
- ¾ teaspoon coconut flour
- ¼ teaspoon organic baking powder
- 1/8 teaspoon Italian seasoning
- Pinch of salt

Dip

- ¼ cup mayonnaise
- Pinch of garlic powder
- Pinch of ground black pepper

Directions:

1. Preheat a mini waffle iron and then grease it.
2. For chaffles: In a medium bowl, put all ingredients and with a fork, mix until well combined. Place half of the

mixture into preheated waffle iron and cook for about 3–4 minutes.

3. Repeat with the remaining mixture.
4. Meanwhile, for dip: in a bowl, mix together the cream and stevia.
5. Serve warm chaffles alongside the dip.

Nutrition:

Calories 248 Net Carbs 1.2 g Total Fat 24.3 g Saturated Fat 4.9

g Cholesterol 98 mg Sodium 374 mg Total Carbs 1.g Fiber 0.4 g Sugar 0.2gProtein 5.9 g

Chaffles With Chocolate Balls

Preparation time: 9 minutes

Servings:2

Cooking Time: 5 Minutes

Ingredients:

- 1/4 cup heavy cream
- ½ cup unsweetened cocoa powder
- 1/4 cup coconut meat

CHAFFLE Ingredients:

- 1 egg
- ½ cup mozzarella cheese

Directions:

1. Make 2 chaffles with chaffle ingredients.
2. Meanwhile, mix together all ingredients in a mixing bowl.
3. Make two balls from the mixture and freeze in the freezer for about 2 hours until set.
4. Serve with keto chaffles and enjoy!

Nutrition:

Protein: 18% 46 kcal Fat: 78% 196 kcal Carbohydrates: 4% 10 kcal

Garlic Bread Chaffle

Preparation time: 9 minutes

Cooking Time: 15 Minutes

Servings: 2

Ingredients:

- 1 tbsp + 1 tsp almond flour
- 1 egg
- ¼ tsp baking powder
- ½ tsp garlic powder
- 1/8 tsp Italian seasoning
- 1 tbsp finely chopped cooked beef liver
- ¼ tsp garlic salt
- 3 tsp unsalted butter (melted)
- ½ cup shredded mozzarella cheese
- 2 tbsp shredded parmesan cheese

Garnish:

- Chopped green onion

Directions:

1. Preheat the oven to 375°F and line a baking sheet with parchment paper.
2. Plug the waffle maker to preheat it and spray it with non-stick spray.

3. In a mixing bowl, combine the almond flour, baking powder, Italian seasoning, garlic powder, beef liver and cheese. Add the egg and mix until the ingredients are well combined.
4. Fill the waffle maker with appropriate amount of the batter and spread the batter to the edges of the waffle maker to cover all the holes on the waffle iron.
5. Close the lid of the waffle maker and cook for about 3 to 4 minutes or according to waffle maker's settings.
6. Meanwhile, whisk together the garlic salt and melted butter in a bowl.
7. After the cooking cycle, remove the chaffle from the waffle iron with a plastic or silicone utensil.
8. Repeat step 4, 5 and 7 until you have cooked all the batter into chaffles.
9. Brush the butter mixture over the face of each chaffle.
10. Top the chaffles with parmesan cheese and arrange them into the line baking sheet.
11. Place the sheet in the oven and bake for about 5 minutes or until the cheese melts.
12. Remove the bread chaffles from the oven and leave them to cool for a few minutes.
13. Serve warm and top with chopped green onions.

Nutrition:

Fat 18g 23% Carbohydrate 4.5g 2% Sugars 0.9g Protein 12g

Cauliflower Hash Brown Chaffle

Preparation time: 9 minutes

Cooking Time: 8 Minutes

Servings: 2

Ingredients:

- 1 egg
- ½ cup cauliflower rice
- ¼ tsp onion powder
- ¼ tsp salt
- ½ tsp garlic powder
- 4 tbsp shredded cheddar cheese
- 1 green onion (chopped)

Directions:

1. Put the cauliflower rice in a microwave safe dish and cover the dish. Place the dish in the microwave and microwave for 3 minutes.
2. Remove the dish from the microwave and stir. Return it to the microwave and steam for about 1 minute or until tender.
3. Let the steamed cauliflower cool for a few minutes. Wrap the steamed cauliflower in a clean towel and squeeze it to remove excess water.
4. Plug the waffle maker to preheat it and spray it with a non-stick cooking spray.

5. In a mixing bowl, combine the cauliflower, green onion, onion powder, cheese, salt, garlic and salt. Add the egg and mix until the ingredients are well combined.
6. Fill your waffle maker with an appropriate amount of the batter and spread out the batter to cover all the holes on the waffle maker.
7. Close the waffle maker and cook until the chaffle is browned. This will take about 4 minutes or more depending on your waffle maker.
8. After the cooking cycle, use a plastic or silicone utensil to remove the chaffle from the waffle maker.
9. Repeat step 6 to 8 until you have cooked all the batter into waffles.
10. Serve the hash brown chaffles and top with your desired topping.

Nutrition:

Fat 6.9g 9% Carbohydrate 2.9g 1% Sugars 1.2g Protein 7.1g

Bacon Jalapeno Popper Chaffle

Preparation time: 10 minutes

Cooking Time: 10 Minutes

Servings: 2

Ingredients:

- 4 slices bacon (diced)
- 3 eggs
- 3 tbsp coconut flour
- 1 tsp baking powder
- ¼ tsp salt
- ½ tsp oregano
- A pinch of onion powder
- A pinch of garlic powder
- ½ cup cream cheese
- 1 cup shredded cheddar cheese
- 2 jalapeno pepper (deseeded and chopped)
- ½ cup sour cream

Directions:

1. Plug the waffle maker to preheat it and spray it with a non-stick cooking spray.
2. Heat up a frying pan over medium to high heat. Add the bacon and saute until the bacon is brown and crispy.
3. Use a slotted spoon to transfer the bacon to a paper towel lined plate to drain.

4. In a mixing bowl, combine the coconut flour, baking powder, salt, oregano, onion and garlic.
5. In another mixing bowl, whisk together the egg and cream cheese until well combined.
6. Add the cheddar cheese and mix. Pour in the flour mixture and mix until you form a smooth batter.
7. Pour an appropriate amount of the batter into the waffle maker and spread the batter to the edges to cover all the holes on the waffle maker.
8. Close the waffle maker and cook for about 5 minutes or according to waffle maker's settings.
9. After the cooking cycle, use a plastic or silicone utensil to remove the chaffle from the waffle maker.
10. Repeat step 7 to 9 until you have cooked all the batter into chaffles.
11. Serve warm and top with sour cream, crispy bacon and jalapeno slices.

Nutrition:

Fat 51g 65% Carbohydrate 13.5g 5% Sugars 2.1g Protein 30.6g

Apple Pie Chaffle

Preparation time: 9 minutes

Cooking Time: 6 Minutes

Servings: 2

Ingredients:

- 1 egg (beaten)
- 1 tbsp almond flour
- 1 big apple (finely chopped)
- 1 tbsp heavy whipping cream
- 1 tsp cinnamon
- 1 tbsp granulated swerve
- ½ tsp vanilla extract
- 1/3 cup mozzarella cheese

Topping:

¼ tbsp sugar free maple syrup

Directions:

1. Plug the waffle maker and preheat it. Spray it with non-stick spray.
2. In a large mixing bowl, combine the swerve, almond flour, mozzarella, cinnamon and chopped apple.
3. Add the eggs, vanilla extract and heavy whipping cream. Mix until all the ingredients are well combined.

4. Fill the waffle maker with the batter and spread out the batter to the edges of the waffle maker to all the holes on it.
5. Close the lid of the waffle maker and cook for about 4 minute or according to waffle maker's settings.
6. After the cooking cycle, remove the chaffle from the waffle maker with a plastic or silicone utensil.
7. Repeat step 4 to 6 until you have cooked all the batter into chaffles.
8. Serve and top with maple syrup.

Nutrition:

Fat 7.8g 10% Carbohydrate 1 7% Sugars 12.1g Protein 5.4g

Keto Gingerbread Chaffle

Preparation time: 9 minutes

Cooking Time: 8 Minutes

Servings: 2

Ingredients:

- 1 egg (beaten)
- 1/8 tsp garlic powder
- ¼ tsp nutmeg
- ½ tsp cinnamon
- ½ cup shredded mozzarella cheese
- 2 tsp granulated swerve
- ½ tsp baking powder
- 2 tbsp almond flour
- ½ tsp ginger

Topping:

- ½ cup heavy cream
- 1 tsp cinnamon
- 1 tsp sugar free maple syrup

Directions:

1. Plug the waffle maker to preheat it and spray it with a non-stick cooking spray.
2. In a medium mixing bowl, combine the almond flour, baking powder, cinnamon, garlic, ginger, nutmeg, swerve

and cheese. Add the egg and mix until the ingredients are combined.

3. Pour an appropriate amount of the batter into the waffle maker and spread out the batter to the edged to cover all the holes on the waffle maker.
4. Close the waffle maker and cook for about minutes or according to your waffle maker's settings.
5. After the cooking cycle, use a plastic or silicone utensil to remove the chaffle from the waffle maker.
6. Repeat step 2 to 5 until you have cooked all the batter into waffles. Let the chaffles sit for a few minutes to cool.
7. For the filling, combine the heavy cream, cinnamon and syrup in a mixing bowl. Mix until smooth and fluffy.
8. Top the chaffles with the cream mixture and serve.

Nutrition: Fat 18.2g 23% Carbohydrate 6.8g 2% Sugars 0.6g Protein 7g

French Toast Chaffle Sticks

Servings: 8

Cooking Time: 40 Minutes

Ingredients:

- 6 organic eggs
- 2 cups mozzarella cheese, shredded
- ¼ cup coconut flour
- 2 tablespoons powdered erythritol
- 1 teaspoon ground cinnamon
- 1 tablespoon butter, melted

Directions:

1. Preheat your oven to 350°F and line a large baking sheet with a greased piece of foil.
2. Preheat a waffle iron and then grease it.
3. In a bowl, add 4 eggs and beat well.
4. Add the cheese, coconut flour, erythritol and ½ teaspoon of cinnamon and mix until well combined.
5. Place ¼ of the mixture into preheated waffle iron and cook for about 6–8 minutes.
6. Repeat with the remaining mixture.
7. Set the chaffles aside to cool.
8. Cut each chaffle into 4 strips.
9. In a large bowl, add the remaining eggs and cinnamon and beat until well combined.
10. Dip the chaffle sticks in the egg mixture evenly.

11. Arrange the chaffle sticks onto the prepared baking sheet in a single layer.
12. Bake for about 10 minutes.
13. Remove the baking sheet from oven and brush the top of each stick with the melted butter.
14. Flip the stick and bake for about 6–8 minutes.
15. Serve immediately.

Nutrition:

Calories 96 Net Carbs 1.5 g Total Fat 6.3 g Saturated Fat 2.9 g Cholesterol 130 mg Sodium 99 mg Total Carbs 3.2 g Fiber 1.7 g Sugar 0.3 g Protein 6.7 g

Sweet Brownie Chaffle

Preparation time: 9 minutes

Cooking Time: 14 Minutes

Servings: 2

Ingredients:

- 1 large egg
- ¼ tsp baking powder
- ½ tsp vanilla extract
- ½ tsp ginger
- 2 tbsp cream cheese (melted)
- 1 ½ tsp cocoa powder
- 1 tbsp swerve

Topping:

- ½ tsp vanilla extract.
- ½ tsp cinnamo
- ¼ tsp liquid stevia
- 2 tbsp heavy cream
- 6 tbsp cream cheese (melted)

Directions:

1. Plug the waffle maker to preheat it and spray it with a non-stick cooking spray.
2. In a mixing bowl, combine the swerve, cocoa powder, ginger and baking powder.

3. In another mixing bowl, whisk together the cream cheese, egg and vanilla.
4. Pour the cocoa powder mixture into the egg mixture and mix until the ingredients are well combined.
5. Fill the waffle maker with an appropriate amount of batter and spread the batter to the edges to cover all the holes on the waffle maker.
6. Close the waffle maker and cook for about 7 minutes or according to your waffle maker's settings.
7. After the cooking cycle, use a silicone or plastic utensil to remove the chaffle from the waffle maker. Set aside to cool completely
8. Repeat step 5 to 7 until all the batter has been cooked into chaffles.
9. For the filling, combine the vanilla, cream cheese, stevia, cinnamon and heavy cream in a mixing bowl. Mix until well combined.
10. Spread the cream frosting over the surface of one chaffle and cover with another chaffle.
11. Place the filled chaffles in a refrigerator and chill for about 15 minutes.
12. Serve and enjoy.

Nutrition:

Fat 22.2g 28% Carbohydrate 3.8g 1% Sugars 0.6g Protein 6.8g

Savory Chaffle Stick

Preparation time: 5 minutes 6

Cooking Time: 25 Minutes

Servings: 2

Ingredients:

- 6 eggs
- 2 cups shredded mozzarella cheese
- A pinch of salt
- ½ tsp ground black pepper or to taste
- ½ tsp baking powder
- 4 tbsp coconut flour
- 1 tsp onion powder
- 1 tsp garlic powder
- 1 tsp oregano
- ¼ tsp Italian seasoning
- 1 tbsp olive oil
- 1 tbsp melted butter

Directions:

1. Plug the waffle maker to preheat it and spray it with a non-stick cooking spray.
2. Break 4 of the eggs into a mixing bowl and beat. Add the coconut flour, baking powder, salt, cheese and Italian seasoning. Combine until the ingredients are well combined. Add more flour if the mixture is too thick.

3. Pour an appropriate amount of the batter into the waffle maker and spread out the batter to cover all the holes on the waffle maker.
4. Cover the waffle maker and cook for about 7 minutes or according to your waffle maker's settings. Make sure the chaffle is browned.
5. After the cooking cycle, use a plastic or silicone utensil to remove the chaffle form the waffle maker.
6. Repeat step 3 to 5 until you have cooked all the batter into chaffles.
7. Cut the chaffles into sticks. Each mini chaffle should make about 4 sticks.
8. Preheat the oven to 350°F. Line a baking sheet with parchment paper and grease it with the melted butter.
9. Break the remaining two eggs into another mixing bowl and beat.
10. In another mixing bowl, combine the oregano, pepper, garlic and onion.
11. Dip one chaffle stick into the egg. Bring it out and hold it for a few seconds to allow excess liquid to drip off.
12. Dip the wet chaffle stick into the seasoning mixture and make sure it is coated with seasoning. Drop it on the baking sheet.
13. Repeat step 11 and 12 until all the chaffle sticks are coated.
14. Arrange the chaffle sticks into the baking sheet in a single layer.
15. Place the baking sheet in the oven and bake for 10 minutes.
16. Remove the baking sheet from the oven, brush the oil over the sticks and flip them.
17. Return it to the oven and bake for an additional 6 minutes or until the stick are golden brown.

18. Remove the sticks from the oven and let them cool for a few minutes.
19. Serve and enjoy.

Nutrition:

Fat 4.1g 5% Carbohydrate 2g 1% Sugars 0.2g Protein 3.4g

Keto Avocado Chaffle Toast

Preparation time: 5 minutes

Cooking Time: 8 Minutes

Servings: 2

Ingredients:

Avocado Topping:

- 1 tbsp butter
- 1 green bell pepper (finely chopped)
- ½ cup feta cheese
- ½ avocado
- 1 tsp lemon juice
- ¼ tsp nutmeg
- ¼ tsp onion powder
- ½ tsp ground black pepper or to taste

Chaffle:

- ½ mozzarella cheese
- 1 egg (beaten)
- 1 tbsp Almond flour
- 1 tsp cinnamon
- ½ tsp baking soda

Directions:

1. Plug the waffle maker tom preheat it and spray it with a non-stick spray.
2. In a mixing bowl, combine the mozzarella, almond flour, baking soda and cinnamon. Add the egg and mix until the ingredients are well combined and you form a smooth batter.
3. Fill the waffle maker with appropriate amount of the batter and spread the batter to the edges of the waffle maker to cover all the holes on the waffle iron.
4. Close the lid of the waffle maker and cook for about 3 to minutes or according to waffle maker's settings.
5. Meanwhile, dice the avocado into a bowl and mash until smooth. Add the bell pepper, nutmeg, onion powder, ground pepper and lemon juice. Mix until well combined.
6. After the baking cycle, remove the chaffle the waffle maker with a silicone or plastic utensil.
7. Repeat step 3, 4 and 6 until you have cooked all the batter into chaffles.
8. Brush the butter over the chaffles. Spread the avocado mixture over the chaffles. Top with shredded feta cheese.
9. Serve and enjoy.

Nutrition:

Fat 68.6g 88% Carbohydrate 31g 11% Sugars 11.5g Protein 29.8g

Green Chaffle

Preparation time: 5 minutes

Cooking Time: 8 Minutes

Servings: 2

Ingredients:

- 4 tbsp finely shredded cabbage
- 2 eggs (beaten)
- 1/3 cup shredded mozzarella cheese
- 1 slice of bacon (finely chopped)
- A pinch of salt
- 1 tsp tamari sauce
- 1 tbsp chopped green onion
- 1/8 tsp ground black pepper or to taste

Topping:

- 1 tbsp kewpie mayonnaise or American mayonnaise
- 2 tbsp bonito flakes
- 2 tsp Worcestershire sauce

Directions:

1. Heat up a frying pan over medium to high heat and add the chopped bacon.
2. Sear until the bacon is brown and crispy. Use a slotted spoon to transfer the bacon to a paper towel lined plate to drain.

3. Plug the waffle maker to preheat it and spray it with a non-stick spray.
4. In a mixing bowl, combine the crispy bacon, cabbage, cheese, onion, pepper and salt. Add the egg and tamari. Mix until the ingredients are well combined.
5. Pour an appropriate amount of the batter into the waffle maker and spread out the batter to cover all the holes on the waffle maker.
6. Close the waffle maker and cook for about 4 minutes or according to your waffle maker's settings.
7. After the cooking cycle, use a silicone or plastic utensil to remove the chaffle from the waffle maker.
8. Repeat step 5 to 7 until you have cooked all the batter into chaffles.
9. Top the chaffles with sauce, mayonnaise and bonito flakes.
10. Serve warm and enjoy.

Nutrition:

Fat 23.3g 30% Carbohydrate 9.1g 3% Sugars 4.3g Protein 22.9g

Zucchini Chaffles On Pan

Servings:4

Cooking Time:5minutes

Ingredients:

- 1 cup zucchini, grated
- 1 egg
- 1 cup cheddar cheese
- pinch of salt
- 1 tbsp. avocado oil

Directions:

1. Heat your nonstick pan over medium heat.
2. Pour salt over grated zucchini and let it sit for 5 minutes Utes.
3. Remove water from zucchini
4. In a small bowl, mix zucchini, egg, and cheese together.
5. Grease pan with avocado oil.
6. Once the pan is hot, pour 2 tbsps. zucchini batter and cook for about 1-2 minutes Utes.
7. Flip and cook for another 1-2 minutes Utes.
8. Once the chaffle is brown, remove from pan.
9. Serve coconut cream on top and enjoy.

Nutrition:

Protein: 21% 42 kcal Fat: 77% 153 kcal Carbohydrates: 2% 3 kcal

Blt Chaffle Sandwich

Preparation time: 5 minutes

Cooking Time: 10 Minutes

Servings: 2

Ingredients:

Sandwich Filling:

- 2 strips of bacon
- A pinch of salt
- 2 slices tomato
- 1 tbsp mayonnaise
- 3 pieces lettuce

Chaffle:

- 1 egg (beaten)
- ½ cup shredded mozzarella cheese
- ¼ tsp onion powder
- ¼ tsp garlic powder
- ½ tsp curry powder

Directions:

1. Plug the waffle maker and preheat it. Spray it with a non-stick spray.
2. In a mixing bowl, combine the cheese, onion powder, garlic and curry powder. Add the egg and mix until the ingredients are well combined.

3. Fill the waffle maker with the batter and spread the batter to the edges of the waffle maker to cover all the holes on the waffle iron.
4. Close the lid of the waffle maker and cook for about minutes or according to waffle maker's settings.
5. After the cooking cycle, remove the chaffle from the waffle maker using a silicone or plastic utensil.
6. Repeat step 3 to 5 until you have cooked all the batter into chaffles. Set the chaffles aside to cool.
7. Heat up a skillet over medium heat. Add the bacon strips and sear until all sides of the bacon is browned, turning and pressing the bacon while searing.
8. Use a slotted spoon to transfer the bacon to a paper towel lined plate to drain.
9. Place the chaffles on a flat surface and spread mayonnaise over the face of the chaffles.
10. Divide the lettuce into two and layer it on one portion on both chaffles.
11. Layer the tomatoes on one of the chaffles and sprinkle with salt. Layer the bacon over the tomatoes and place the other chaffle over the one containing the bacon.
12. Press and serve immediately. Enjoy!!!

Nutrition:

Fat 30g 39% Carbohydrate 7.8g 3% Sugars 2.7g Protein 18.4g